Woodland Fauna

Level 5 – Green

Helpful Hints for Reading at Home

The graphemes (written letters) and phonemes (units of sound) used throughout this series are aligned with Letters and Sounds. This offers a consistent approach to learning, whether reading at home or in the classroom.

HERE IS A LIST OF NEW PHONEMES FOR THIS PHASE OF LEARNING. AN EXAMPLE OF THE PRONUNCIATION CAN BE FOUND IN BRACKETS.

Phase 5			
ay (day)	ou (out)	ie (tie)	ea (eat)
oy (boy)	ir (girl)	ue (blue)	aw (saw)
wh (when)	ph (photo)	ew (new)	oe (toe)
au (Paul)	a_e (make)	e_e (these)	i_e (like)
o_e (home)	u_e (rule)		

Phase 5 Alternative Pronunciations of Graphemes			
a (hat, what)	e (bed, she)	i (fin, find)	o (hot, so, other)
u (but, unit)	c (cat, cent)	g (got, giant)	ow (cow, blow)
ie (tied, field)	ea (eat, bread)	er (farmer, herb)	ch (chin, school, chef)
y (yes, by, very)	ou (out, shoulder, could, you)		

HERE ARE SOME WORDS WHICH YOUR CHILD MAY FIND TRICKY.

Phase 5 Tricky Words			
oh	their	people	Mr
Mrs	looked	called	asked
could			

TOP TIPS FOR HELPING YOUR CHILD TO READ:

- Allow children time to break down unfamiliar words into units of sound and then encourage children to string these sounds together to create the word.
- Encourage your child to point out any focus phonics when they are used.
- Read through the book more than once to grow confidence.
- Ask simple questions about the text to assess understanding.
- Encourage children to use illustrations as prompts.

This book focuses on /oe/ and /au/ and is a Green level 5 book band.

Can you sort all the words on this page into two groups?

Foe

Aloe

Words with oe

Hoe

Paunch

Sauna

Words with au

Launch

Exhaust

Have you ever been to the woods? If you have, you might have seen some woodland fauna. Fauna means animals.

Woods

You might spot some animals if you tiptoe in and keep still. Do not stomp or you will spook them.

Keep alert. Can you hear or see an animal near you? They might be on the lookout for food.

If you see a big animal saunter past, it could be a doe or a buck.

If it has antlers, it might be a buck. If there are no antlers, it might be a doe.

Bucks shed their antlers, but they come back as the year goes on. The antlers will come back bigger than they were when they dropped off.

If you see a flash of auburn as a little animal goes past, it could be lots of different things.

It could be a fox or a squirrel. They both have tails with lots of fur on them.

Squirrel

Fox

If you cannot see an animal near you, you can check for tracks in the mud.

Different woodland animals have different feet. You can tell what an animal is from just one print!

If you see a print from a long, cleft hoof, it might be from a buck or doe.

Cleft hoof

If you see a print with little toes, it might be from a fox, skunk or raccoon... or you!

©2023 **BookLife Publishing Ltd.**
King's Lynn, Norfolk, PE30 4LS, UK.

ISBN 978-1-80505-063-6

All rights reserved. Printed in China.
A catalogue record for this book is
available from the British Library.

Woodland Fauna
Written by Charis Mather
Designed by Lucy Otter

An Introduction to BookLife Readers...

Our Readers have been specifically created in line with the London Institute of Education's approach to book banding and are phonetically decodable and ordered to support each phase of the Letters and Sounds document.

Each book has been created to provide the best possible reading and learning experience. Our aim is to share our love of books with children, providing both emerging readers and prolific page-turners with beautiful books that are guaranteed to provoke interest and learning, regardless of ability.

BOOK BAND GRADED using the Institute of Education's approach to levelling.

PHONETICALLY DECODABLE supporting each phase of Letters and Sounds.

EXERCISES AND QUESTIONS to offer reinforcement and to ascertain comprehension.

CLEAR DESIGN to inspire and provoke engagement, providing the reader with clear visual representations of each non-fiction topic.

AUTHOR INSIGHT:
CHARIS MATHER

Charis Mather is a children's author at BookLife Publishing who has a love for reading and writing. Her studies in linguistics and experiences working with young readers have given her a knack for writing material that suits a range of ages and skill levels. Charis is passionate about producing books that emphasise the fun in reading and is convinced that no matter how much you already know, there is always something new to learn.

PHASE 5
/oe/au/

This book focuses on /oe/ and /au/ and is a Green level 5 book band.

Image Credits Images are courtesy of Shutterstock.com. With thanks to Getty Images, Thinkstock Photo and iStockphoto. Cover – Alfmaler, Andrew Pustiakin, Eric Isselee, ONYXprj. 4–5 – Blaj Gabriel, Lea Cabrera. 6–7 – Pressmaster, WildMedia. 8–9 – Szymon Bartosz, WildMedia. 10–11 – Erik Mandre, Menno Schaefer, Vaclav Sebek. 12–13 – Marina Demidiuk, PepeQuilez. 14–15 – Purino, Steve Simkins.